SECRETS
OF THE
ANIMAL WORLD

CHEETAHS
Fleetest of Foot

by Eulalia García
Illustrated by Gabriel Casadevall and Ali Garousi

Gareth Stevens Publishing
A WORLD ALMANAC EDUCATION GROUP COMPANY

Please visit our web site at: www.garethstevens.com
For a free color catalog describing Gareth Stevens Publishing's
list of high-quality books and multimedia programs,
call 1-800-542-2595 or fax your request to (414) 332-3567.

The editor would like to extend special thanks to Richard Sajdak, Aquarium and Reptile Curator, Milwaukee County Zoo, Milwaukee, Wisconsin, for his kind and professional help with the information in this book.

Library of Congress Cataloging-in-Publication Data

García, Eulalia.
   [Guepardo. English]
   Cheetahs: fleetest of foot / by Eulalia García; illustrated by Gabriel Casadevall and
Ali Garousi.
      p. cm. – (Secrets of the animal world)
   Includes bibliographical references (p. 31) and index.
   Summary: Describes the physical characteristics, behavior, unique abilities, feline
relatives, and threats to survival of the cheetah.
   ISBN 0-8368-1495-9 (lib. bdg.)
   1. Cheetah–Juvenile literature. [1. Cheetah.] I. Casadevall, Gabriel, ill. II. Garousi,
Ali, ill. III. Title. IV. Series.
QL737.C23G3613   1996
599.74'428–dc20   95-54164

This North American edition first published in 1996 by
Gareth Stevens Publishing
A World Almanac Education Group Company
330 West Olive Street, Suite 100
Milwaukee, Wisconsin 53212 USA

This U.S. edition © 1996 by Gareth Stevens, Inc. Created with original © 1993
Ediciones Este, S.A., Barcelona, Spain. Additional end matter © 1996 by Gareth
Stevens, Inc.

Series editor: Patricia Lantier-Sampon
Editorial assistants: Jamie Daniel, Diane Laska, Rita Reitci

Printed in the United States of America

2 3 4 5 6 7 8 9 06 05 04 03 02

CONTENTS

THE CHEETAH'S WORLD

The cheetah family

Cheetahs are carnivorous mammals that belong to the Felid, or cat, family. Felines live in the wild all over the world except in Madagascar, Australia, and Antarctica. Almost every continent has its own dangerous feline predators: in Africa, the lion is king; in Asia, the tiger; in South America, the puma and the jaguar; in North America, the puma; in Africa and southern Asia, the leopard, or panther. The lynx lives in Europe and North America. Cheetahs live in Africa and in the Near East, in flat country where they have plenty of room to stalk and hunt prey.

This cheetah is alert because it senses movement in its territory.

The cheetah eats its prey quickly before another carnivore tries to take it away.

Earth's fastest mammal

The cheetah is built for speed. Its body is slim and sleek, and its long, thin legs enable it to run up to 70 miles (113 kilometers) per hour. This makes it one of the most feared predators of the African savanna and the fastest mammal on Earth. When the cheetah locates its prey, it stares at its victim and prepares itself for the strike. The cat moves in slowly, and after each movement stops to make sure the other animal has not spotted it. With muscles tensed, the predator calculates the distance and runs toward its prey for a lightning-fast strike. The prey runs off in terrified surprise, with its enemy closing in. After a short chase, the cheetah catches its prey and sinks its teeth into the animal's neck.

Sleek figure, long legs, belly sunk inward, small head, and spotted coat — unmistakable. The cheetah is the fastest animal on Earth.

The cheetah is a feared hunter. On the open plains, it watches its prey from afar.

The fastest of the felines

The felines are fast-moving predators that stalk and ambush when they hunt. The lion is the best-known feline. The male has a thick mane that becomes longer and darker with age. When chasing prey, the lion can reach speeds of up to 34 miles (55 km) per hour, although it is usually the lioness that hunts for food to feed the pride. The largest feline is the Siberian tiger; an adult male can weigh more than 660 pounds (300 kg). The tiger can run quickly after

All the cats on this page stalk their prey and trap them after a short chase.

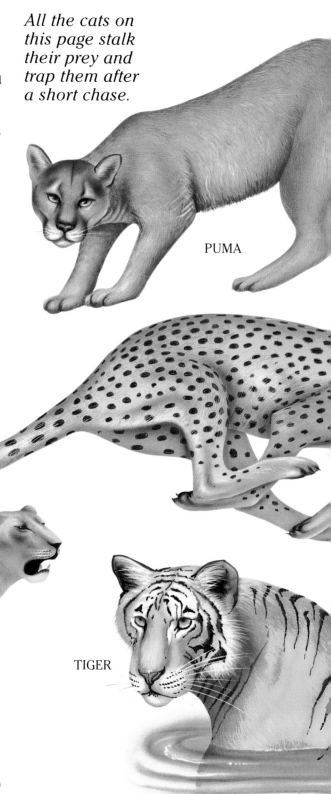

PUMA

LIONESS

TIGER

6

LEOPARD

CHEETAH

LYNX

prey, which it brings down through sheer force of weight, then holds with great paws to tear apart with its teeth. The puma has no markings on its skin and is the most common large feline in North and South America. The lynx has triangular ears with tufts of black hair. The leopard can hunt animals much larger than itself. It stalks prey for a long time, then captures it after a short, quick chase. The cheetah is the only feline that depends on its great speed rather than its strength to trap prey.

INSIDE THE CHEETAH

BRAIN

EYES
Eyes are placed high up on the head. They are very large, with round pupils that can focus perfectly on prey. Since it hunts mostly during the daylight hours, its day vision is much better than its night vision.

LUNGS
The cheetah starts quickly and reaches its maximum speed within a few yards (m). The lungs can move quickly from 60 to 150 breaths per minute.

ESOPHAGUS

RIBS

LIVER

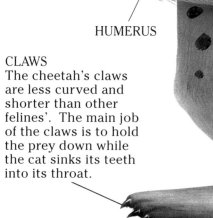

HEAD
The head is small and lightweight, and does not slow the animal down. Its nose is lined with two dark stripes that connect the eyes to both sides of the mouth.

CANINES
Sharp, pointed canine teeth grow from the upper jaw along small channels that lead to the inside of the nose. The cheetah can breathe with prey in its teeth.

TRACHEA

HUMERUS

CLAWS
The cheetah's claws are less curved and shorter than other felines'. The main job of the claws is to hold the prey down while the cat sinks its teeth into its throat.

Thanks to its lightweight body and powerful muscles and tendons, the cheetah can reach a speed of 50 miles (80 km) per hour in only a few seconds, and up to 70 miles (113 km) per hour. The cheetah's heart, lungs, and blood vessels are larger than normal to withstand sudden, violent movements.

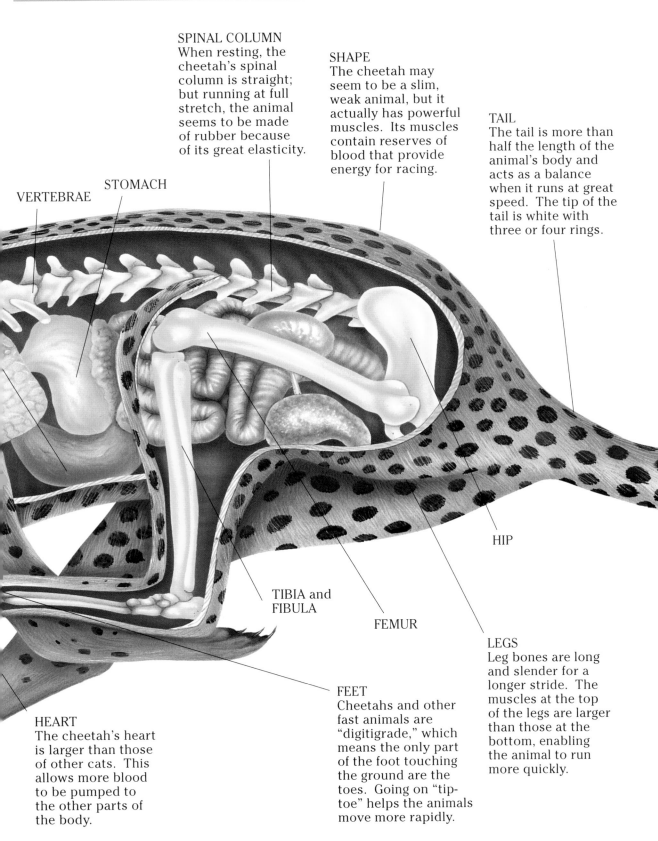

SPINAL COLUMN
When resting, the cheetah's spinal column is straight; but running at full stretch, the animal seems to be made of rubber because of its great elasticity.

SHAPE
The cheetah may seem to be a slim, weak animal, but it actually has powerful muscles. Its muscles contain reserves of blood that provide energy for racing.

TAIL
The tail is more than half the length of the animal's body and acts as a balance when it runs at great speed. The tip of the tail is white with three or four rings.

VERTEBRAE

STOMACH

HIP

TIBIA and FIBULA

FEMUR

LEGS
Leg bones are long and slender for a longer stride. The muscles at the top of the legs are larger than those at the bottom, enabling the animal to run more quickly.

FEET
Cheetahs and other fast animals are "digitigrade," which means the only part of the foot touching the ground are the toes. Going on "tip-toe" helps the animals move more rapidly.

HEART
The cheetah's heart is larger than those of other cats. This allows more blood to be pumped to the other parts of the body.

9

THE SWIFT CHEETAH

Champion runner

If the cheetah competed with other animals in contests of speed, it would always win the gold medal. Its body is built for incredible speed. Its long, slender legs give it the huge strides that, in seconds, take it to its prey. In full stride, the cheetah's body is actually off the ground for most of the time and touches only for tenths of a second — just long enough to propel the cheetah forward again without seeming to touch the ground.

The cheetah's strides are so long it seems to float in the air.

A mother cheetah and her cubs look for shade to cool themselves in the heat of the savanna.

With each stride, the cheetah propels itself forward using its back legs. Then it seems to fly through the air with legs and body fully stretched. It lands on its front legs ready to propel itself forward again. If you watch a cheetah in slow motion, its entire body acts like a spring extending and contracting in rhythm to the movements of the legs. Running this quickly is important to the cheetah because its principal sources of food are mammals, such as gazelles and antelopes, that also move very rapidly. It bites or seizes prey by the throat after a sprint of a few yards (m) and asphyxiates, or suffocates, them.

After a strong start, the cheetah covers the distance that separates it from its prey in only a few seconds.

that cheetahs do not retract their claws like other cats?

If you have a cat at home, you know that it likes to sharpen its claws, and that there are times when the claws cannot be seen or felt. When the cat doesn't need its claws, it can retract, or pull them in, like most felines and hide them under a covering of skin. It pulls the claws out to scratch, climb, or hold down its prey. The cheetah cannot pull its claws in completely, so they are always partly visible.

The running machine

The cheetah starts running with an amazing burst of speed that allows it to reach its maximum speed of up to 70 miles (113 km) per hour in only five or six seconds. But it can do this for only a short period of time. If it does not reach its target in 330 to 660 feet (100 to 200 m), it has to give up in order to regain its strength. The cheetah chooses its prey carefully, and it is not distracted from its target by other nearby animals.

The cheetah climbs on fallen tree trunks or rocks to get a full view of its hunting grounds.

The cheetah's speed allows it to catch the swift gazelles of the vast African savannas.

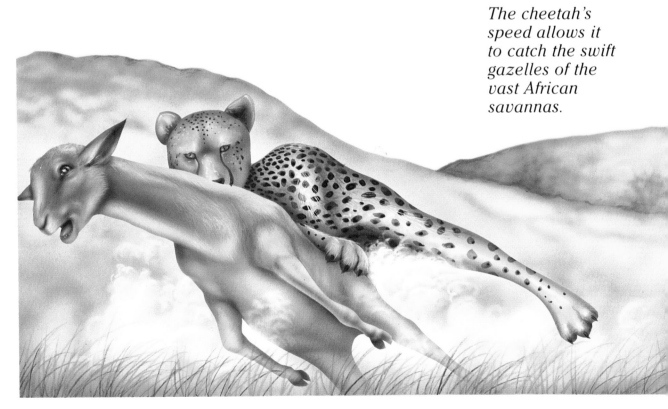

CHEETAHS AND OTHER HUNTERS

Two lionesses watch a herd of zebras before attacking.

The stalking hunters

The cheetah's hunting tactics are simple. First, it waits and watches silently for a few minutes or up to an hour. A short chase of about twenty seconds follows; it rarely runs for more than one minute. When stalking prey, the cheetah approaches cautiously with its head down, unlike other cats that stay crouched to get as near as possible. Cheetahs normally hunt alone, but may join others from the same litter to capture bigger prey. Lions and lionesses, however, normally hunt in teams. Leopards stalk their prey; when the prey is only a short distance away, the leopard runs toward it, trapping and carrying it to a tree to eat. Many felines hunt at night or in late evening. The large, sensitive whiskers and the magnificent night vision that the majority of them have make it easy for them to spot prey in the dark. Cheetahs, however, only hunt during the daytime, at times when other felines are not very active.

Leopards normally carry their captured prey into a tree to eat.

Two lionesses approach a herd from different sides. The victim of the attack is an old, sick zebra that has been lagging behind.

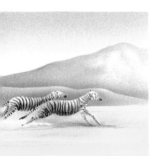

that cheetah cubs have mohawks?

Many felines have spots or patches on their coats. These marks act as camouflage and help them get close to their prey without being noticed. Cheetah cubs are born with spots and a short, spiky, blue-gray mane down their necks. This makes them look fierce to other animals and prevents them from being attacked. This bright head of hair also helps their mother find her cubs in the long grasses of the plains.

The great lone hunters

With long, narrow stripes that disguise its shape, a lone, male Bengal tiger silently stalks a wild pig. From its hiding place, the tiger advances until its target is only a few feet (m) away. It decides to attack, then launches its 500-pound (225-kg) body forward. After two or three giant leaps, it lands on its prey.

The jaguar is also a solitary hunter. Its robust body, short, stocky legs, and enormous canine teeth make it one of the most powerful felines. It is the only feline that regularly hunts reptiles, such as turtles and alligators.

Jaguars live in the jungle near rivers, where they can trap capybaras, turtles, and alligators.

The tiger has a voracious appetite. It eats more than one ton of meat a year.

THE FIRST FELINES

The history of felines

Felines are descended from mammals that lived some 55 million years ago. They had long bodies, small brains, and the ability to live in trees.

These felines evolved into silent, stealthy hunters with deadly canine teeth and sharp claws. Not all of them survived: for example, the saber-toothed cat became extinct almost 10,000 years ago. Smilodon was called a saber-tooth because of its huge upper canine teeth, which were almost 6 inches (15 cm) long and as sharp as sabers. Smilodon's teeth were serrated at the back, and it had to open its mouth wide to bite its prey. Its most common prey were mastodons and bison. Saber-toothed cats often left the remains of their victims lying

around because they would not risk breaking their canines on the hard bones. This provided food for other animals as well as the first humans. Other primitive cats included cave cats that were the largest felines ever — even larger than the Siberian tiger.

Primitive Homotherium may have looked like this. It had shorter canine teeth than the saber-tooth, but was equally deadly to its prey.

To avoid breaking its huge canine teeth, Smilodon may have killed prey by sinking them into the softest parts of its victim's body.

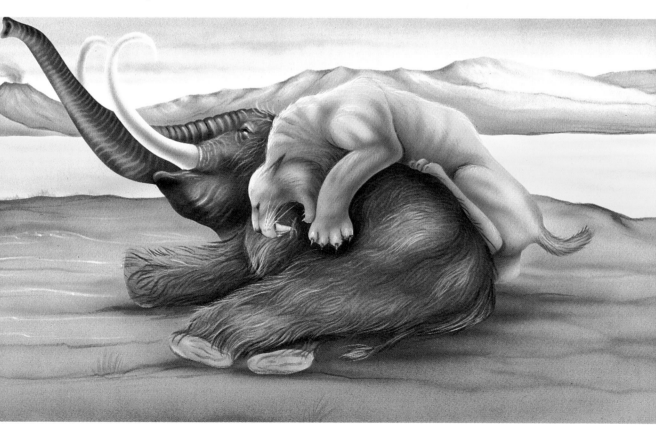

that cheetahs were trained to hunt?

Cheetahs are easy to tame, and humans have long admired their speed. The emperors of India used cheetahs for racing. In the Middle East and India, cheetahs were used to hunt gazelles or hares. The cheetahs were led on a leash and set free to hunt on cue. These cheetahs hunted not out of instinct, but out of hunger, because they usually had not been fed for days.

HUNTING BEHAVIOR

First hunting lessons

The mother cheetah cares for her cubs until they are fourteen to eighteen months old. When the cubs first leave the den, they travel with their mother to hunt. To teach the cubs, the mother captures small animals without killing them. She sets the prey free in front of the cubs. The youngsters then try to catch the prey. The cubs are usually impatient at first. They jump too hastily, often leaping clear over their prey. This gives the little animal time to run away.

Cheetah cubs enjoy playing chase and fighting. These activities help them learn to hunt and defend themselves.

The mother cheetah brings prey to her cubs so they can learn to stalk and trap prey on their own.

In danger of extinction

The cheetah is endangered for several reasons. Its habitat is being reduced by humans who want the land for agriculture and grazing. A few thousand years ago, the cheetahs came close to extinction. Inbreeding by the survivors left the animals open to sickness. In a litter of seven cubs, just two to four live more than three months. Only the mothers feed and care for the cubs. If they leave to find food, the cubs are at risk from attacks by hyenas and other big cats.

Cheetahs are sensitive to infections. Many cubs die before they are three months old.

Females give birth to their cubs in hidden lairs or dens.

The small hunters

Lynxes are swift hunters of rodents and hares. They have strong legs, a short tail, thick beards, and ears tipped with plumes of hair that appear to help their hearing. Servals live on the African plains. They have long necks and enormous ears, like bats, with which they explore their territory. They stalk their prey before attacking. If the prey escapes, they follow, leaping on all fours as if bouncing on a trampoline.

Servals use their keen sense of hearing to find prey. This is why, unless they are very hungry, they do not hunt on a windy day.

The lynx is built for running over snow after its prey. Its paws are covered in thick hair.

APPENDIX TO

SECRETS
OF THE
ANIMAL WORLD

CHEETAHS
Fleetest of Foot

CHEETAH SECRETS

▼ **Mortal combat.** Male cheetahs can either live separately or in groups called coalitions. When outsiders try to invade their territory, they defend it to the death.

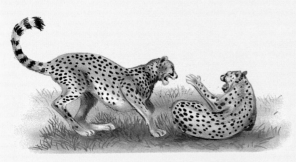

▼ **Marking their territory.** The cheetah expels urine on the trunk of a tree. This is to mark its territory and warn off any intruders.

The cheetah and the zoo. Cheetahs have more difficulty reproducing in captivity than most cats because of their social structure and low male fertility. With improved understanding, however, reproduction in zoos has become more common.

▼ **The dry plains or savanna.** Most carnivores need to drink often. The cheetah is an exception because it has adapted to the dry plains. It can last up to ten days without drinking.

Gentle puppies. Cheetah cubs are like gentle puppies; even adults rarely try to bite, unlike a trapped leopard or tiger.

Motherly love. Having few ways of defending her young, a mother cheetah protects her cubs by making sure other predators do not see her when she returns to the den.

▶ **King cheetah.** Once thought to be a different species, the king cheetah of South Africa has a strange coat. Many of its spots join to form stripes!

1. Where do cheetahs live?
a) Australia.
b) All over America.
c) Africa or the Near East.

2. The most common large feline in North and South America is:
a) the lynx.
b) the puma.
c) the serval.

3. What is the maximum speed of a cheetah?
a) Up to 70 miles (113 km) per hour.
b) Up to 50 miles (80 km) per hour.
c) Up to 35 miles (55 km) per hour.

4. Which is the largest cat?
a) The cheetah.
b) The Siberian tiger.
c) The lion.

5. What do leopards do with their prey?
a) Take them up a tree to eat.
b) Leave them for other animals.
c) Keep them and cover them with earth.

6. With each stride, the cheetah propels itself forward with its:
a) back legs.
b) front legs.
c) heavy tail.

The answers to CHEETAH SECRETS questions are on page 32.

GLOSSARY

adapt: to change behavior or adjust needs in order to survive in changing conditions.

ambush: a surprise attack made from a hidden position.

asphyxiate: to suffocate or choke so that breathing is impossible.

calculate (v): to estimate or solve the meaning of.

camouflage: a way of disguising someone or something to make it look like its surroundings. A cheetah's spots help it blend in with its habitat.

canine teeth: sharp, pointed teeth in front of an animal's mouth, used for tearing off pieces of meat or other tough food.

capybara: a large, tailless South American rodent. Capybaras are often more than 4 feet (1.2 m) long.

carnivore: an animal that eats meat as its source of food.

continents: the large landmasses of Earth, which include Africa, Antarctica, Asia, Australia, Europe, North America, and South America.

contract (v): to pull in and make smaller or shorter.

crouch: to lower the body into a squatting position.

den: the lair or shelter of a wild animal.

digitigrade: walking on the toes (digits) rather than on the bottoms of the feet; most quadrupeds, or four-footed animals, are digitigrade.

esophagus: the tube inside the body that connects the throat to the stomach so food can pass into it.

evolve: to change or develop gradually from one form to another. All living things change and adapt to survive or they can become extinct.

extinct: no longer in existence.

feline: belonging to, related to, or characteristic of the cat family.

habitat: the natural home of a plant or animal.

herds: large groups of animals that

graze and live together as protection against predators.

inbreeding: mating and bearing offspring between animals that are closely related. Inbreeding cheetahs leaves the animals vulnerable to sickness.

instinct: a pattern of activity or tendency that is inborn.

lair: the den or home of a wild animal.

litter: a group of animals born to one mother at the same time.

mammals: warm-blooded animals that have backbones. Female mammals produce milk to feed their young.

mane: long, thick hair around or at the back of the neck of some animals, such as lions.

mastodon: an elephant-like animal, now extinct, that had larger teeth and tusks than present-day elephants.

predators: animals that kill and eat other animals.

prey: animals that are hunted and killed for food by other animals.

pride: a group of lions that live and hunt together.

primitive: of or relating to an early and usually simple stage of development.

propel: to move in a forward direction.

pupil: the opening in the center of the eye through which light enters.

reptiles: a group of cold-blooded animals that have backbones, crawl on the ground, and have scaly skin.

retract: to pull in or withdraw. Most members of the cat family can retract their claws.

rodents: a group of mammals with large front teeth for gnawing. Beavers, mice, rats, and squirrels are rodents.

saber: a heavy military sword with a curved blade. The saber-toothed cat's teeth resembled this sword.

savanna: a flat landscape or plain usually covered in coarse grasses and scattered trees.

serrated: having a jagged or zig-zag edge.

sleek: smooth and shiny; well-groomed.

solitary: alone; isolated.

species: animals or plants that are closely related and often similar in behavior and appearance. Members of the same species can breed together.

sprint: a run at top speed for a short distance.

stalk: to track or follow in a quiet, secretive manner.

stealthy: slow and secretive.

stride: a long step.

tendons: tough cords or bands of tissue that connect muscle to bone.

vast: huge in size; immense.

vertebrae: small, interconnected segments of bone that make up the spinal column.

visible: in full view; able to be seen or identified.

voracious: very hungry; having a huge appetite.

ACTIVITIES

◆ Visit a zoo and try to get "eye to eye" with a cheetah. What do the cheetahs and other big cats at the zoo eat? What special needs do big cats in captivity have? How has the zoo tried to recreate their natural habitat? Do cheetahs adapt easily to zoo life? Do they reproduce well in captivity?

◆ Use an old, large cardboard box as your base and art supplies such as poster paint, markers, glue, and cardboard to construct a savanna habitat like the ones cheetahs live in naturally. Paint the inner sides of the box a bright blue for the sky and add a hot, orange sun. Use dry grass or straw to make grassland and twigs to make trees. Cut foliage from construction paper. Be sure to include a water source. Use clay or plasticine to make cheetahs and other animals to inhabit your savanna. Don't forget to provide your cheetahs with prey!

MORE BOOKS TO READ

African Animals Discovery Library. Six volumes. Lynn Stone (Rourke)

African Landscapes. Warren J. Halliburton (Macmillan)

Big Cats. Markus Kappeler (Gareth Stevens)

Big Cats. Jenny Markert (Facts on File)

Cheetah. ALC Staff (Morrow)

Cheetahs. Jenny Markert (Childs World)

Discover African Wildlife: Activity Book. Laura C. Beattie (Carnegie)

Extremely Weird Endangered Species. Sarah Lovett (John Muir)

Lions and Tigers. Joanne Mattern (Troll Associates)

Small Cats. Markus Kappeler (Gareth Stevens)

To Run Like the Wind: or the Wisdom of the Cheetah. Nelson A. Marco (Twenty-Fifth Century Press)

Trumpa the Cheetah. Edward Zingg (Abdo & Daughters)

VIDEOS

Animals of Africa: Big Cats of the Kalahari. (Just for Kids Home Video)

The Big Cats: Endangered Predators. (Britannica Films)

Cheetah. (Britannica Films)

On the Edge of Extinction: Panthers and Cheetahs. (National Audubon Society Video)

PLACES TO VISIT

The Museum of Comparative Zoology
26 Oxford Street
Cambridge, MA 02138

The Santa Barbara Museum of Natural History
2559 Puesta del Sol Road
Santa Barbara, CA 93105

Royal Melbourne Zoological Gardens
Elliott Avenue
Parkville, Victoria
Australia 3052

Wellington Zoo
Newtown
New Zealand

Granby Zoo
347 Bourget Street
Granby, Quebec
J2G 1E8

African Lion Safari and Game Farm
Cambridge, Ontario
N1R 5S2

INDEX